# Creative Ideas for Bridal and Baby Showers

by **Darlene Hoffa**

**illustrated by Diane Johnson**

STANDARD PUBLISHING
Cincinnati, Ohio

Unless otherwise noted, all Scripture quotations are taken from the HOLY BIBLE: NEW INTERNATIONAL VERSION, copyright ©1978 by the New York International Bible Society. Used by permission of Zondervan Bible Publishers.

Library of Congress Cataloging-in-Publication Data

Hoffa, Darlene.
　Creative ideas for bridal and baby showers.

1. Showers (Parties)　　2. Entertaining.　　I. Title.
GV1472.7.S5H64　1987　　　793.2　　　86-23156
ISBN 0-87403-224-5

Copyright ©1987. The STANDARD PUBLISHING Company, Cincinnati, Ohio. A division of STANDEX INTERNATIONAL Corporation.
Printed in U.S.A.

# Contents

Introduction . . . . . . . . . . . . . . . . . . . . . . . . . . . . . . . . . . . 5

Plan 1 – How to Grow a Husband . . . . . . . . . . . . . . . . . . . 9

Plan 2 – The Art of Building a Marriage . . . . . . . . . . . . . . 13

Plan 3 – Recipe for a Happy Ever-after . . . . . . . . . . . . . . 19

Plan 4 – Something Old, Something New . . . . . . . . . . . . 23

Plan 5 – Your Baby: a Work of Art . . . . . . . . . . . . . . . . . . 29

Plan 6 – Mary Had a Little Lamb . . . . . . . . . . . . . . . . . . . 35

Plan 7 – A Star Is Born . . . . . . . . . . . . . . . . . . . . . . . . . . 42

Baby Shower Interview Questions . . . . . . . . . . . . . . . . . . 49

Bridal Shower Interview Questions . . . . . . . . . . . . . . . . . 51

Gift Opening Ideas . . . . . . . . . . . . . . . . . . . . . . . . . . . . . 53

Recipes . . . . . . . . . . . . . . . . . . . . . . . . . . . . . . . . . . . . . 55

# Introduction

Is someone you know getting married or expecting a baby? Give her a shower that she'll remember! *Creative Ideas for Bridal and Baby Showers* will show you how to plan a fun-filled party for all who come. Be ready to have a good time yourself, and enjoy Christ's presence from start to finish. A creative shower, planned lovingly for your honored guest, may become one of her most treasured gifts.

While Scripture is silent on the subject of showers, we know that Jesus participated in several celebrations during his ministry. In fact, his first miracle occurred at a wedding in Cana. John 2:1-11 records the compelling drama.

When the merrymaking outlasted the refreshments, Jesus' mother summoned him to help. Transforming ordinary water into wine, Jesus "saved the day."

A close look at this miracle unveils a story bubbling with richness, much like the wine pouring from the earthen jars. Jesus' actions reached far beyond ensuring a successful party for a young couple. His intervention expressed His blessing on life's happy times when they honor Him as Lord.

The story of the wedding at Cana provides the basic principles used in this book. These shower plans are lighthearted and fun, yet filled with deep meaning. The four principles include

1. Use of familiar themes,
2. Group participation,
3. Concern for everyone present, and
4. Sharing Christ-centered messages.

**Use of Familiar Themes**

While some of the customs at the Cana festivity differ from today's traditions, the main participants are familiar. The story captures our attention because it deals with a setting we recognize and understand.

Each shower plan also centers on a familiar theme. Gardening, home-building, and cooking are examples. Name tags, decorations, and refreshments reinforce each central idea. The most powerful emphasis of the theme emerges in the devotional messages. Everyone will experience a well-planned time from start to finish.

## Group Participation

When the refreshments ran out at the Cana celebration, Jesus activated a dramatic chain of events. His mother, the servants, and banquet host joined as partners in Jesus' first miracle. Each shower plan also encourages group participation.

*Name Tags*

Unique name tags invite guests to interact more freely. Recalling names after first-time introductions is difficult for most of us. Even lifelong friends' names can prove elusive at times. Name tags remedy this situation. Conversations begin and continue more frequently when guests can link names and faces with a glance.

*Non-Competitive Activities*

Activities, based on small-group techniques, are designed to bring people together. Creative ideas for giving advice to the guest of honor is one method. Groups often include personalities ranging from clown to saint. A colorful mixed bouquet of counsel emerges as helpful hints blossom from this variety of sources. The wise bride- or mother-to-be can gather wisdom from everyone.

Another type of activity uses interviews for group involvement. Most shower guests are delighted to learn more about the guest of honor's anticipated event. A variety of interview formats will entertain and enlighten those present. Guests may add interesting pieces of information as the interviews progress. The result will be a warm atmosphere of fun.

*Concern Shown for Everyone Present*

When Jesus changed water into wine, the honored couple, guests, and host all experienced Jesus' loving concern for people. The bridal couple's honor remained intact, and the guests' celebration continued. The wedding banquet host, a first century caterer, retained his integrity in the community. This book features this same type of caring for people. The bride- or mother-to-be, guests, and hostess are all shown consideration in the plans.

*Concern for Guest of Honor*
Your honoree will occupy 'center stage' as others learn of her experiences and future plans. The value others place on her happiness can be sensed through her carefully planned shower, as well as by the gifts she receives.

*Concern for Invited Guests*
Concern for guests is expressed through involving them in activities. They will enjoy the friendly atmosphere, and the refreshments which are suitable for everyone, whether feasting of fasting.

*Concern for Hostess*
The hostess, also, is considered in the shower plans. From props for devotional messages to decorations, most items are available in discount stores. Some may be borrowed from friends or found at home. Both the hostess' bank account and time budget are in safekeeping.

**Sharing Christ-centered Messages**
The celebration at Cana shines from Scripture because it signaled the beginning of Jesus' miracles. More than water yielded to His touch. Lives changed as they met Him!

Each of the shower plans carries the message of Jesus' life-changing power. While the devotionals speak directly to the guest of honor, everyone is a learner in the area of relationships, especially in marriage and motherhood. God's word is the greatest source of wisdom for both.

The devotional messages are based on Scripture, outlined with sound psychological principles, and sprinkled with humor. Presented with love, and backed with prayer, each devotional message is equipped to carry spiritual truths deep into the hearts of listeners.

If someone you know is getting married or expecting a baby, give her a shower to remember. Choose a theme she'll enjoy. Surround her with loving friends. Prepare to enjoy the party yourself. And be sure to invite Jesus, asking Him to bless this event as He did the celebration long ago in Cana.

# 1
# How to Grow a Husband

**Theme Verse:** "And now just as you trusted Christ to save you, trust him, too, for each day's problems; live in vital union with him. Let your roots grow down into him and draw up nourishment from him. See that you go on growing in the Lord, and become strong and vigorous in the truth you were taught. Let your lives overfow withjoy and thanksgiving for all he has done." – Colossians 2:6, 7 (The Living Bible)

**Decorations:** This bridal shower is ideal for spring and summer weddings when garden flowers are plentiful. Scatter bouquets of mixed flowers in light pastels around the room. Arrange a larger bouquet on the serving table. Weave a wreath of flowers for the bride's hair or pin a single flower on her clothing.

If flowers are not available, purchase several packs of small blooming plants at a nursery. Wrap the containers in tissue paper. Tie pastel ribbons around them. Crystal and china serving pieces add an elegant touch, or you may substitute paper goods in spring colors.

**Name Tags:** Cut 2" x 3" rectangles of pastel construction paper. Purchase one package of gift wrap paper with a floral design. Cut out single flowers and glue on each name tag. Write names with felt-tip pen. Secure with double-sided tape.

**Activity 1: The Bride Is Like a Red, Red, Rose.**

Give each guest a pen and a sheet of paper. Ask the guests to write the flower which most closely resembles the bride and why. Encourage humorous as well as serious responses. Collect answers and read them aloud. Keep contributors' names anonymous until the bride selects her favorite. Make a keepsake for the bride by tying the answers together with ribbon to place in her bridal book.

## Activity 2: Love's in Bloom.

Select ten to fifteen questions from the Bridal Shower Interview Questions, on page 51, which are appropriate to ask this bride. Write each question on a small piece of paper, roll up, and tie with a ribbon to the branches of a blooming, potted plant or a green houseplant. Let guests untie them, one at a time, and ask the bride each question. Encourage others to add information to the bride's answers.

## Devotional Message: How to Grow a Husband

(Bride's Name), the (Name of Church) Garden Club met today because we heard that you are soon going to start growing a husband. Many brides assume everyone has a matrimonial green thumb. We're here to tell you that husband growing is an exotic art. Please excuse me while I don my gardening clothes, and we'll get down to the roots of this matter. (Put on a colorful apron, gardening gloves, and a large, floppy hat.)

**The Container:** (Place an attractive pot on the table.)

(Bride's Name), the first step in growing a husband is choosing the right container. While you may get away with almost anything the first few months of your marriage, when the bloom starts to fade a bit, husbands tend to notice where they are planted! This container, which represents your new home's environment, can become the perfect spot for your 'husband-growing' endeavor.

Over the years, our Garden Club members have found that shiny, cheery, containers work best. As (Groom's Name)'s wife, you can provide this type of atmosphere by being fun to live with, relaxed, and comfortable in everyday situations, always expecting something good to emerge from whatever happens.

While we hope your husband won't resemble Felix Unger of The Odd Couple, we find most husbands do appreciate some semblance of neatness when it comes to their surroundings. Some are even willing to help maintain a degree of order. Give liberal amounts of sunshine and water, in the form of sincere gratitude, if this occurs. Husbands rarely continue household chores which are unnoticed or unappreciated!

(Bride's Name), Our Garden Club members believe you'll be a prize-winner in the "Beauty of Container" category. Use your own creativity, along with your wedding gifts to make your new home sparkle. You'll discover china washes as easily as stoneware, and silver looks better if it's used often! Candles radiate a romantic mood and hide dust simultaneously. Other men may start to ask (Groom's Name) where he found such a woman!

A husband grows like a weed in a container of this kind. Cultivating a life-style of beauty shows the man you love that he is important, your favorite guest, and your most cherished friend.

**The Soil:** (Show guests a bag of commercial potting soil and place some of it in a container.)

(Bride's Name), your next step for growing a husband is furnishing the right soil. The best place for a bride to nourish her husband is in the soil of God's Word. (Read Colossians 2:6, 7, The Living Bible.) This Scripture can be a constant source of wisdom as you learn to be a good wife. These verses recommend that you come to the Lord with your problems, decisions, and differences of opinions, better known to seasoned 'gardeners' as fights. Your shared faith and respect for God's Word will give you a common ground and goal. You will discover a never-ending supply from which to draw nourishment for your marriage.

**Care and Feeding:** (Place a small plant in the container.)

Growing a husband, requires more precise care and feeding

than any other plant in your garden. A husband may appear to be a sturdy oak, but will remain that way with proper care.

(Groom's Name) will depend on you to be the primary giver of psychological nourishment in your relationship. Women, since the beginning of time, have cared for the people they love. Continue this age-old tradition with your husband. Feed him with affirmation, encouragement, empathy, and kindness. If he starts to droop around the edges, apply some plant food: run off to a hotel with him for a weekend, write him a love letter and hide it in his lunch or briefcase, or buy him a favorite cologne with a catchy name to make him smile. Give excellent care to your husband every day God gives you together.

**Results:** (Display plant and container to guests and bride.)

Few projects will give you as great a return for your effort as growing a husband. First of all, love that is cultivated in someone you love almost always multiplies, coming back a thousandfold to the giver. Second, you may grow more beautiful yourself, since you share the same environmental conditions. Best of all, you and (Groom's Name) can present a refreshing garden to your family and friends, proving that God's idea of marriage can flourish in today's world.

**Prayer:** Dear Father, thank You for bringing (Bride's Name) and (Groom's Name) together. Bless their marriage with the sunshine of Your presence. Nourish their love that it may grow through the years. In Jesus' name, Amen.

Present the plant to the bride with a typed or handwritten copy of the devotional message for her bridal book.

**Open Gifts:** (See Gift Opening Ideas, page 53.)

**Refreshments:** Lemon Angel Food Dessert (page 60)
　　　　　　　　Assorted Vegetable Tray with Herbal Dips (page 57)
　　　　　　　　Sparkling White Grape Punch (page 56)
　　　　　　　　Coffee and Tea (decaffeinated and regular)

# 2
# The Art of Building a Marriage

**Theme Verse:** "The wise woman builds her house." — Proverbs 14:1 (NIV)

**Decorations:** Use earth and sky tones for serving table linens and crepe paper streamers. Choose stoneware or paper dishes. On the table place a small doll house with furniture which guests may rearrange. Dress two dolls as a bride and groom. The doll house may be as simple as a cardboard box or as elaborate as a Victorian model.

**Name Tags:** Cut 2" x 3" rectangles of light blue paper. Cut houses, as shown, from brown paper. Glue in place. Add small balls of cotton for puffs of smoke. Write names with dark blue felt-tip pen. Attach with double-sided tape.

**Refreshments:** Provide a variety of greens and salad ingredients. Include a selection of toppings and salad dressings for a build-your-own salad bar. Serve bran and orange muffins, citrus punch, tea, and coffee (decaffeinated and regular).

**Activity 1: Meet the Bride**

Select ten to twenty questions from the Bridal Interview Questions on page 51, which are suitable for this bridal couple. Pass a pen and paper to each guest and the bride. Have the group number their papers according to the number of questions you will ask. As you ask each question, request both bride and guests to write an answer. After completing the quiz, go through questions, comparing the bride's correct answers with those of the group. Guesses or fictitious answers offered by the guests add to the merriment. Give a small gift to the person whose answers most closely correspond with the bride's.

**Activity 2: The Happy-Homemaker Game**

Make a book cover, which will be a large version of the name tags, by folding an 8½" x 11" sheet of light blue construction paper in half. Add a house with small puffs of cotton by the chimney to represent smoke. Cut typing paper in half to make pages for the book.

Pass out a pen and a page to each guest. Ask everyone to write a household hint for the bride. These can be serious or silly. Collect the papers and read aloud. Give a small gift for the bride's favorite page. Enclose hints in the cover to add to the bride's bridal book.

**Preparation for the Devotional Message:** Bring a large brimmed hat, oversized dress and purse, ornate beads, and a fake fur or shawl.

Cut simple house sections and sun from construction paper. Background size should be determined by the size of the room and the number of guests. Make background 16" x 20" or larger, using sturdy paper such as poster board which will stand on an easel or be held up by your assistant. Color suggestions: blue background, brown foundation, white house, yellow windows and door, and red roof. Organize sections of

house so they can be easily found during the message. Ask a friend to tape the sections in place. Double-sided or regular cellophane tape can be used. Dress in dress-up clothes as you speak.

## Devotional Message: The Art of Building a Marriage

(Bride's Name), do you remember playing house when you were a little girl? You gathered your dolls, dress-up clothes, and play dishes. Then you corrraled a boy cousin or neighbor to be your pretend husband.

An hour or two, and a terrible mess, later, the oversized clothes and miniature muffin pans went back in the toy box. Mother called you to a *real* supper, and your little playmate went happily home to his trucks and trains.

Most young girls love to play house. Unfortunately, many adults follow the same rules when creating a real home.

God has other ideas. Throughout Scripture, marriage is compared to a house, worthy of His presence, and deserving our best efforts to build and preserve it.

My assistant carpenter, (Name), and I are going to construct a prefab house before your very eyes! There's an art to building this house today, but a far greater skill is needed in building a marriage. God's blueprints promise success to you and (Groom's Name) if you follow these instructions.

The basic structure, like any house, needs a foundation, walls, windows, doors, and a roof. Get ready now for some marvelous building skills.

**Foundation:** (Hand construction-paper foundation to assistant to tape on the lower section of the background. Hold up for everyone to see the first step.)

The first step for any structure is a foundation. Unless you want to slide out of bed one morning because the floor has acquired a forty-five degree angle, you must give your house a solid footing. Marriage also requires a firm foundation. Psalm 127:1 declares, "Unless the Lord builds the house, its builders labor in vain." (Groom's Name)'s and your relationship to Jesus Christ is the basic, vital beginning for a strong marriage. A solid, mutual faith offers purpose, a common loyalty, and eternal value to your commitment to each other. You will see substitute foundations advertised everywhere such as money, education, and travel. These can enhance a marriage, but are worthless as a foundation.

**Walls:** (Hand your assistant the wall section to tape above the foundation. Display to guests.)

As you see, we are very speedy builders.

Walls in God's plans for marriage represent commitment to each other. Walls of commitment announce to the world that you and (Groom's Name) have decided to love each other as long as you both shall live. Walls of commitment say that you and (Groom's Name) are Number One with each other and want no one as Number Two! Walls of commitment say you and (Groom's name) do not consider each other a starter house, to stay with five years, until school is completed or careers are established. Walls of commitment declare that you and (Groom's Name) want to be a permanent twosome as long as God allows you to live, love, and laugh together.

Although the basic walls remain permanently secured in place in God's plan for marriage, you may find yourselves repainting or rewallpapering them many times. This signifies growth, change, and vitality. Your personalities may change during the coming years. The key for success in building a marriage lies in growing together, not apart. In the midst of healthy change, keep your basic commitment strong and stable throughout your entire marriage.

**Doors and Windows:** (Tape windows and door in place, and show to guests.)

Our prefab company offers doors and windows which are not only instantaneous, but also come fully curtained. A cheery welcome mat is also included!

Doors and windows in your marriage represent the people who will come and go in your lives. They represent the boys and girls, men and women whom you'll teach in Sunday school, counsel in youth groups, or invite for an overnight stay. People can bring freshness to a marriage, opening you to the fun of loving others in Jesus' name.

Having open hearts doesn't require holding "Open House" twenty-four hours a day. Extended, continuous hospitality soon changes to drudgery. Our construction company recommends your marriage house close all doors and windows at least one or two nights a week to other occupants. Rest, relaxation, and recreation are essential to the overall soundness of the house you will build together.

**Roof:** (Tape in place and show guests.)

This last addition is extremely important!

The roof must completely cover the house since it represents the protection which marriage partners give each other. Storms occur in the lives of all people, whether they are believers or not. Storms arrive in the shape of illness, accidents, or the daily grind of hard work. The Bible says that two are better than one in many situations. For instance, Ecclesiastes 4:9-12 records the benefit of a partner when working on a project, when a helping hand is needed, when the night is cold, or when a burglar attacks!

Teamwork builds a storm-tight roof on your marriage. Be <u>(Groom's Name)</u>'s encourager, affirmer, and self-esteem protector. Be his partner and best friend. Be his sweetheart and pal.

Proverbs 14:1 (NIV) suggests, "The wise woman builds her house. "<u>(Bride's Name)</u>, reinforce the foundation of your faith. Make sure it's strong. Build walls of solid commitment to stay together. Throw open the doors and windows of your home to others, to love them in Jesus' name. Roof your marriage tightly, so it will withstand the fiercest of storms. God's smile will be upon you, His loving Presence (Add sun in sky above house.) blessing each day of your marriage.

**Prayer:** Father, thank You for bringing (Bride's and Groom's Names) together. As they build a house of marriage, supply Your blessing and guidance. Help them keep their commitment to each other and to the people You will send them to love. Shelter them all the days of their lives with Your presence. In Jesus' name, amen.

Present a typed or handwritten copy of the devotional message to the bride.

**Open Gifts:** (See Gift Opening Ideas on page 53.)

**Refreshments:** Pineapple-Carrot Cake (page 62)
Raw Vegetable Bouquet with Crab Dip (page 58)
Assorted Crackers
Sparkling White Grape Punch (page 56)
Coffee and Tea (decaffinated and regular)

# 3
# Recipe for a Happy Ever-after

**Theme Verse:** "Be kind and compassionate to one another, forgiving each other, just as in Christ God forgave you. Be imitators of God, therefore, as dearly loved children, and live a life of love, just as Christ loved us." – Ephesians 4:32 – 5:2 (NIV)

**Decorations:** Arrange brown and white crepe paper streamers around the serving table. Fashion a bouquet of wooden spoons or kitchen tools in a basket or brown bowl. Tie brown and white checked bows on each tool and a larger bow on the container. Complete the bouquet by filling in between the utensils with baby's breath. Place on a serving table. Use white linens and brown napkins.

**Name Tags:** Cut 2″ x 3″ rectangles of white construction paper. Draw a pair of his and her wooden spoons as shown. Glue tiny brown and white checked bows on handles. Write names with a brown felt-tip pen. Secure with double-sided tape.

## Activity 1: Joy of Cooking up a Happy Marriage

Pass out a recipe card and a pen to each guest. Ask everyone to write her recipe for a happy marriage. Encourage humorous as well as serious advice. Collect cards and read aloud without revealing names of authors. Give a small gift to contributor of bride's choice. Place "recipes" in recipe box for a keepsake for the bride.

## Activity 2: The Way to a Man's Heart

Ask guests to share experiences of the first time they cooked a meal for their husbands or boyfriends. Avoid going around the room in a circle for this game. Allow volunteers to participate, rather than pressure everyone to contribute.

**Preparation for the Devotional Message:** You will need a chef's hat, apron, mixing bowl, egg beater, chocolate instant pudding mix, milk in a measuring cup, and dessert dishes. Ask a volunteer to be assistant chef if you find it difficult to speak and mix the ingredients at the same time.

Slip into the hat and apron as the devotional begins, and introduce your assistant.

**Devotional Message: Recipe for a Happy Ever-after**
(Bride's Name), brides-to-be are sometimes like spotless new dish towels, quite inexperienced around the kitchen of matrimony. I've created a little recipe to help you whip up a happy marriage.

This fail-proof recipe comes from God's Word. Read Ephesians 4:32 – 5:2, NIV. In these verses we find the ingredients for a beautiful, fulfilling marriage. Acceptance, forgiveness, and love are three essentials for every wife and husband. God has lovingly placed these ingredients on the shelf of the believer's heart.

**Acceptance:** (Empty package of instant chocolate pudding mix into bowl.)

I'm using chocolate pudding mix to represent the first ingredient, acceptance. Acceptance is an excellent beginning for cooking up a happy marriage.

Your first stages of acceptance occurred as you fell in love with (Groom's Name). Weren't you sometimes surprised how he chose his clothes, ordered food, or spent money? Family backgrounds are rarely, if ever, identical. While your basic values may be the same, in the kitchen of marriage you may discover some culinary surprises. Romans 15:7 (NIV) is the perfect verse to apply when differences surface: "Accept one another, then, just as Christ accepted you, in order to bring praise to God."

For example Steve and Joan are a young couple who have learned the value of acceptance. Steve came from a practical gift-giving family. Joan's family furnished her a highly emotional environment which placed a high priority on feelings and emotional needs. On their first wedding anniversary, Steve announced that his gift for her was waiting in the trunk of his car. Joan jumped for joy! He remembered! It must be huge if it was in the trunk of the car.

When Steve opened the trunk, the lights dimmed on the celebration. Inside were five bags of fertilizer for Joan's garden. That was several years ago. Today, they accept each other's natural inclinations. They also know how the other partner prefers to be shown love.

**Forgiveness:** (Add milk according to package instructions.)

Another vital ingredient for a happy marriage is forgiveness. Forgiveness is the art of keeping the counter top of your relationship with (Groom's Name) wiped clear of bad feelings. Grudges, pouting, long silences, and avoidance have no place in the kitchen of a happy marriage. Forgiveness reflects a Christ-like attitude, for Christ so freely forgave us.

Now, once in a while, (Bride's Name), you'll face a difference of opinion with (Groom's Name). You'll feel entirely right and entirely wronged. The words which make magic ingredients at this point are, "I'm sorry!" A number of legitimate reasons exist for saying, "I'm sorry," even if you don't feel like doing it. You *are* sorry for the red eyes and nose brought on by tears, for the squeezy feeling in your chest because you don't like to fight, or because you'd much rather be cuddling up with (Groom's Name) than seeing him look sad.

When you say "I'm sorry" first, you follow Christ's example of forgiving us first. (Groom's Name) will find it easier to say he's sorry too!

**Love:** (Mix milk and pudding mix in bowl with egg beater, according to package instructions.)

The last, and most important, ingredient for a happy marriage is love. The world can't get enough of it and neither can your marriage. It's the one ingredient with no limits on the amounts you may add. While too much acceptance or forgiveness can turn one partner into a puppet, love overflows merrily out of a happy marriage, flavoring everyone it touches.

Love (Groom's Name) in thousands of tangible ways. Write him notes and letters. Celebrate dates which are important to your relationship. Plan mini-vacations throughout the year. Keep the sparkle in his eyes by being fun to live with and love.

**Recipe Results:** (Pour pudding mixture into dessert dishes.)

Creating a happy marriage follows many of the same rules as a successful recipe. The right ingredients must be added, in the correct amounts, in a time-tested way. We've talked about three vital ingredients: acceptance, forgiveness, and love. If you practice them faithfully, you'll become an expert cook in the lifelong feast of a joy-filled marriage.

**Prayer:** Dear Father, we thank You for furnishing the recipe for a happy marriage in Your Word. We thank You that Jesus set a loving example of acceptance, forgiveness, and love for (Bride's Name) and (Groom's Name) to follow. In Jesus' name, amen.

**Refreshments:** Chocolate Pudding and Chocolate Dream Cake (page 60)
Fresh Fruit and Cheese (page 59)
Sparkling White Grape Punch (page 56)
Coffee and Tea (decaffeinated and regular)

# 4
# Something Old, Something New

**Theme Verse:** "Lord, you have been our dwelling place throughout all generations. Before the mountains were born or you brought forth the earth and the world, from everlasting to everlasting you are God." – Psalm 90:1, 2 (NIV)

**Decorations:** Recreate an early 1900's setting with a periwinkle blue and white color scheme. Place a handmade quilt, protected by plastic, or a lace tablecloth underlined with blue on the serving table. Arrange mixed bouquets of garden flowers and ferns around the room. Antique serving pieces will add a nostalgic touch. Weave a wreath of baby's breath for the bride's hair. Hostesses may wear long dresses to enhance the mood or borrow a home furnished with antiques for the shower.

**Name Tags:** Make individual nosegays by folding 6" doilies about 1/2" off-center. Glue sides together and add baby's breath or other available flowers in the center. Fasten a blue bow on each nosegay, as shown. Write names with a blue felt pen. Attach with straight pins.

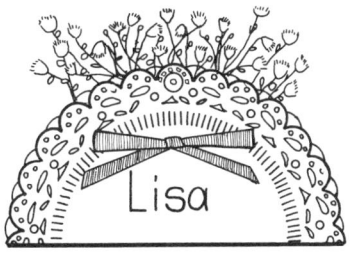

### Activity 1: The Telephone-Party Line

Dress your best actress in old-fashioned garb and have her bustle into the room as the Town Gossip! The Gossip, her speech sprinkled with cliches, will represent the party-line personality who kept track of everyone's business. Explaining that

23

the invention of the telephone encouraged many courtships, she will reveal the party-line phone's *best* feature – several *other* pairs of ears often heard the lover's words too!

Choose 12 to 15 questions from the Bridal Interview Questions (page 51). The Gossip will poll these party-line members to find out how much news they've overheard about this bridal couple! Have the Gossip ask each question, then ask guests to raise their hands if they know the information. The bride can confirm their answers if they are correct.

**Activity 2: Let Me Call You Sweetheart.**

Give each guest a pen and a slip of paper. Ask each person to write something unique about her own courtship or wedding, without telling her identity. These stories can be serious or humorous. Collect answers and read each aloud. Try to match romances with the right sweethearts.

**Preparation for the Devotional Message:** Purchase an inexpensive scrapbook. Make a book cover of white or blue quilted fabric. Glue and sew in place. Add lace and ribbons, if you like. Copy the following format:

Title page:

On page one, write across the top: **Something Old....** In the center of the page glue baby pictures of the Bride and Groom. Across the bottom of the page write, **The Foundation of Your Faith:**

"Lord, you have been our dwelling place throughout all generations. Before the mountains were born or you brought forth the earth and the world, from everlasting to everlasting you are God." – Psalm 90:1, 2 (NIV)

On page two, write across the top: **Something New....** In the center place a recent photo of the bridal couple. At the bottom of the page write the Goethe quote:

"This is the true measure of love,
When we believe we alone can love,
That no one could ever have loved so before us,
And that no one will ever love in the same way after us."
– Goethe

On page three, write across the top: **Something Borrowed....** In the center add a collage of photos of both families' members. Across the bottom of the page write the Scripture verse, 2 Timothy 3:14-16 (NIV).

On page four, write across the top: **Something Blue....** Draw a blue border around the page. Have the guests sign this page with a blue pen as they arrive. Across the bottom of the page write, **Your Commitment**.

**Devotional Message: Something Old, Something New...**

(Bride's Name), our hearts have been 'aflutter' as we've heard about your love story! Of course, we won't mention the news items we've heard about these other women's romances! Maybe party lines should be restored!

I'm sure you're familiar with the age-old tradition of brides carrying something old, something new, something borrowed, and something blue on their wedding day. This special book puts a new face on that old custom. The pages represent

priceless treasures which we believe you'll carry with you into your marriage.
> Something Old – The Foundation of Your Faith
> Something New – Your Love
> Something Borrowed – Your Heritage
> Something Blue – Your Commitment

(Present book to the Bride, suggesting she turn to pages as you ask.)

**Something Old:** *The Foundation of Your Faith*

(Bride's Name), the something old you'll be taking into your marriage is the foundation of your faith! Let's look at that page, first, to see if any *old* things appear! (Let Bride show pictures.)

Old things are finally back in style! *Old* houses are being fixed up. *Old* furniture is being refinished. Even *old* movie and TV stars are receiving important roles and asked their beauty secrets!

Psalm 90:1, 2 tells of something much older and more precious – the timeless God in whom you place your faith. (Read verses aloud.)

You and (Groom's Name) will experience many changes throughout your marriage. People will come and go in your lives. You may work at various jobs and move to a number of homes and cities. In the midst of change, God's *old* unchanging Foundation will be your dwelling place, as it has for all generations.

**Something New:** *Your Love*

You'll also be taking something new into your marriage, your love. We'll look at that page in a moment!

Almost everyone enjoys *new* things! Who can forget the wonder of *new* tennis shoes, *new* Easter outfits, *new* kittens and mittens, and *new*-mown grass? *New* implies a fresh beginning; unchartered territory just waiting for an adventurer!

Let's turn to your Something New page. (Bride can show pictures as you comment about the love-struck pair.) Your *new* love, of course, is better than all the new tennies, outfits, and kittens in the world! *New* love bathes the most ordinary chores in a glow. Everything looks *new* because you hold the most important place in you *new* love's heart. Goethe expressed love this way:

"This is the true measure of love,
When we believe that we alone can love,
That no one could ever have loved so before us, and
That no one will ever love in the same way after us."

(Bride's Name), this newness can last in a marriage which welcomes God's presence. You and (Groom's Name) can happily participate in a lifelong love affair!

**Something Borrowed:** *Your Heritage*

You and (Groom's Name) will each bring something borrowed to your marriage – your family *heritage!* Let's look at those faces on the next page. You're rich!

Borrowing must be one of mankind's top ten ideas. You've probably borrowed your Mother's pans for playing house, your Dad's paintbrushes to redo your room in hot pink, your friend's big brother to scare off unwanted admirers, and your neighbor's ladder to rescue your cat from the roof.

Borrowing comes in handy. No human being's personal inventory can possibly contain *every* item, human or otherwise, which a person needs to have for life's emergencies!

As you walk down the aisle, the values you've borrowed from both of your families will be among your and (Groom's Name)'s most cherished possessions. Your marriage will be enhanced by the blending of these different backgrounds.

Combining two value systems may require a sense of humor and patience, but the result can be even better than the original sources. Young couples whose parents love the Lord are especially blessed. You borrow from a heritage which owns infinite resources. (Read 2 Timothy 3:14-16.)

**Something Blue:** *Your Commitment*

The something blue which you'll carry into your new life will be extremely important in your marriage because blue signifies commitment.

In Numbers 15:38-40, the Israelites were instructed by

Moses to wear a blue cord on the hem of their robes. This blue border signified that God's people were set apart to Him.

(Bride's name), rather than wear blue to express commitment, you and (Groom's Name) can present a picture of Christ and his Bride, the Church, through your marriage. For instance, you can share the joy which bubbles from two hearts who know the Savior. You can demonstrate how disagreements are settled lovingly and show how your commitment to each other is pure and precious and permanent. (Ask bride to turn to page 4.)

This Something Blue page carries the names of your friends who are celebrating with you today. Look back at their signatures often. Remember them as witnesses, this day (today's date) of your commitment to become (Groom's Name)'s wife.

You can fill the remaining pages of your book with memories as the years go by. We're happy that you began with these treasures:
> Something Old – the foundation of your faith;
> Something New – your *love;*
> Something Borrowed – your heritage; and
> Something Blue – your commitment.

**Prayer:** Dear Father, we thank You that from everlasting to everlasting You are God. Recreate the newness of (Bride's and Groom's Names)'s love each day. Honor the heritage they've received from their parents. Fasten the blue cord of commitment about them tightly. Hold them close together in the bonds of love. In Jesus' name, amen.

Present the bride with a typed or handwritten copy of the devotional message.

**Opening Gifts:** (See Gift Opening Ideas on page 53.)

**Refreshments:** Old-fashioned Three-layer Cakes
Fresh Fruit Plate with Hawaiian Adventure Dip (page 58)
Lemonade
Coffee and tea (decaffeinated and regular)

# 5
# Your Baby: A Work of Art

**Theme Verse:** "I praise you because I am fearfully and wonderfully made; your works are wonderful, I know that full well." – Psalm 139:14 (NIV)

**Decorations:** Create the atmosphere of a paint palette in an art studio by forming a canopy of pastel yellow, green, pink, and blue streamers over the serving table. Attach a pastel balloon bouquet to the center of the canopy. Repeat pastel colors in the table linens. Choose paper goods to match.

Make a centerpiece of pink or yellow flowers, artist's brushes, and greenery in a white or copper bowl for the serving table.

**Name Tags:** Cut 3" circles of pastel paper to make a picture frame for each guest. Cut 2 1/2" circles of white paper and glue one in the center of each picture frame. Draw the lower half of a smiling face on each white circle, including eyes, mouth, and ears, as shown. Write guests' names with a pastel felt pen. Provide colored felt-tip pens for guests to add their

own hair color and hairstyle, earrings, and other features to create self-portrait name tags. Attach with straight pins or tape.

### Activity 1: The Impressionist at Work

(Preparation: To make paintbrush handles cut strips of sturdy white paper, 1 1/4 inches x 8 1/2 inches. Cut 2 1/4 inches x 1 1/2 inch pieces of pastel paper to form bristles of brushes. Glue bristles to tips of brushes. Make a paint pot by folding a 12" x 5" piece of yellow construction paper in half. Glue or tape the side edges together).

Give each guest a paper paintbrush and pen. Explain that an artist's work often is an expression of his or her own personality. Ask everyone to write one personality trait of the mother-to-be which they expect to see in her work of art, her baby. These can be humorous or serious. Collect the answers, and read aloud. Place them in the paint pot for the baby's book.

### Activity 2: The Artist Prepares for the Unveiling

Select ten to twelve questions from the Baby Shower Interview Questions on page 49. Ask the mother-to-be the questions, but allow others to add comments.

**Preparation for Devotional Message:** Borrow or simulate an artist's smock, beret, paint palette, brush, canvas, and easel. (Sunday-school rooms often keep easels for visual presentations.) You will also need a 12 inch x 18 inch sheet of light blue paper, a 6 inch smiling face cut from pink paper, a blonde or red paper wisp of hair, and two 1 inch stars. You or an assistant will attach these pieces to the canvas with cellophane tape, as you talk, to form the painting of a baby. The devotional can be attached to the palette for easy reading.

## Devotional Message: Your Baby: a Work of Art

(Mother-to-be's Name), the (Name of Church) Artist's Association recently received a bulletin announcing that *you* are in the midst of a sizeable art project. In fact, we hear it promises to be a *Masterpiece!* So, we're here to cheer you on your way! (Put on beret, set up easel, and hold palette as you speak.) We're always watching for promising artists, and we think you qualify if anyone ever did. (Wave paintbrush in Mother-to-be's direction.)

Creating a work of art, especially on the grand scale of baby, calls for some definite guidelines. Now, (Mother-to-be's name), you can tell by the paint splotches on our shoes (point to shoes) that we don't claim to be *perfect* artists. But we ARE experienced! (Have guests nod in agreement).

Comparing notes, we found several hints which are valuable for both artists and mothers. These are devote time, develop skills, and depend on the Divine Spark.

**Devote Time:** (Mother-to-be's Name), the first essential element of any great art work, especially of a baby, is the artist's willingness to devote a large amount of time to the project. (Put canvas and blue background on easel.) When an artist works on an oil painting, he doesn't take a brush full of paint and go SPLAT, "There's the lake," and SPLAT, SPLAT, "There are two mountains!" (Imitate these motions on the canvas.) Instead, the artist slowly lays a muted wash across the canvas. Shapes remain vague as the foundation for the painting begins. For days, the artist works, adding layer upon layer of pigment. At last, the painter finishes, and viewers are captivated by the richness and depth of his creation.

Your baby will be like a work of art in many ways. Your gifts as an artist can call forth your child's best qualities as you spend days, weeks, and years with him.

Now, when your baby arrives, you'll believe he is absolutely perfect. You'll be overcome with the *Masterpiece* that you and (Father-to-be's Name) have produced! Grandmothers, grandfathers, aunts, uncles, and cousins will support your appraisal. That's why maternity floors have viewing windows! Every baby born is the greatest marvel to hit the planet.

Psalm 139:14 can be paraphrased as the theme song for each baby's arrival, "We praise you because our new baby is fearfully and wonderfully made. Your works (especially this *latest* one) are wonderful. We know *that* full well." (Emphasize italicized words.)

Yet, the proudest parent knows that birth is only the beginning. Time is required for a child to reach his fullest potential physically, psychologically, and spiritually. Time is also needed from the mother to help her little Masterpiece become all God intended him to be.

*Devote* as much *time* as you possibly can to your baby. *Devote time* to bottle-feeding or nursing your child. *Devote time* to singing lullabyes, smiling, talking, and rocking. *Devote time* to playing pat-a-cake, peek-a-boo, and other activities which your baby responds to and loves.

This *time* you devote to your little work of art will produce magnificent results. The colors applied during these early years will vibrate through the finished canvas, delighting you and your child for a lifetime.

**Develop Skills:** (Mother-to-be's Name), the second essential requirement for an artist-mother is to *develop skills*. While a few individuals appear to have talent dropped on them from Heaven, most of us have to work hard to gain a measure of success.

Artist *and* mothers *develop skills* in three major ways: instruction, observation, and experience. (Tape smiling face to background.)

Instruction for creating your work of art is as close as your nearest library. Borrow from the wealth of information already available on child development.

You'll find that while your baby will be one-of-a-kind in some ways, children follow a universal pattern in their developmental stages. This knowledge can save you great concern at times. If, for instance, your baby licks a spot off of the floor when he is one year old, you may avoid panic. Instead nonchalantly remark, "He's normal. One-year-olds learn from taste and touch." You can then rush him to the bathroom to wash out his latest educational adventure. Each day is a new learning experience.

Artists *and* mothers also develop skills by *observation*. If you visit an art studio or gallery, you'll see artists looking over the shoulders of colleagues to see *who* is doing *what* in *which* medium.

Yogi Berra, of baseball fame, advised, "You can observe a lot, just by watching." (Mother-to-be's Name), you can observe a lot, just by *watching!* Find a mother who is willing to teach you what she has learned. Choose a mom whose actions and words declare, "Being the mother of this child, at this time in my life, is the greatest job in the world!"

Artists *and* mothers develop skills, most of all, through *experience*. No matter how many books you've read, or how many mothers you've watched, you will develop skills best through hands on experience. You'll probably be cautious, at first. But after you're sure that your baby won't break on contact, you can relax and enjoy your art project together. Lavish your 'brush strokes' in love upon him. Your mothering skills, blended with your child's temperament and abilities, will produce a unique and priceless 'work of art'.

**Depend on the Divine Spark:** (Mother-to-be's Name), a work of art needs one last element to qualify as a *Masterpiece:* an artist-creator who possesses a divine spark! Michelangelo's Sistine Chapel ceiling and Leonardo da Vinci's Last Supper provide evidence of this phenomenon. Radiating soul-stirring auras, these paintings suggest that their masters surely received a trace of God's creative power: a divine spark.

(Mother-to-be's Name), knowing Jesus Christ personally, you possess far more than a divine spark! Christ lives in your heart through the power of the Holy Spirit. Ephesians 3:20 reveals the source of your inner strength: "Now to him who is able to do immeasurably more than all we ask or imagine, according to his power that is at work within us. (Tape stars on picture over smiling face's eyes to make them 'twinkle'.)

God wants you to use this inner power to become a great mother-artist. He invites you to talk with Him in prayer, and to read His Word each day. Your fellow artists will also be ready to help any time you ask.

As you devote time, develop skills, and depend on the divine spark, your child will become a beautiful 'work of art' – your very own *Masterpiece!*

**Prayer:** Dear Father, You are the Master Artist. Bless the work of art (Mother-to-be's Name) and (Father-to-be's Name) are welcoming into their lives. Splash your color and creativity across their parenting, and into the heart of their little masterpiece. In Jesus' name we pray, amen."

Present the mother-to-be with a typed or handwritten copy of the devotional for her baby's book.

**Open Gifts:** (See Gift Opening Ideas on page 53.)

**Refreshments:** Assorted Open Face Sandwiches
                  Scoops of Sherbet (page 63)
                  Sparkling White Grape Punch (page 56)
                  Coffee and Tea (decaffeinated and regular)

# 6
# Mary Had a Little Lamb

**Theme Verses:** "The Lord is my shepherd, I shall lack nothing. You anoint my head with oil; my cup overflows. Surely goodness and love will follow me all the days of my life, and I will dwell in the house of the Lord forever." – Psalm 23:1, 5, 6 (NIV)

**Decorations:** Set the mood for a Spring Lamb Frolic, although you may use this theme at any time of the year. Use white linens with peach and/or apple green napkins. Fill a wicker basket with houseplants for the serving table. Purchase a stuffed wooly lamb. Tie a large peach bow around lamb's neck and place by the basket. Encircle the lamb and basket with greenery and flowers. Borrow additional toy lambs to scatter around the room. Add peach or green streamers.

**Name Tags:** Cut lambs from heavy white paper. Draw in

details with black felt pen, as shown. Write names in peach or green. Write "Where am I?" in obscure letters on the back of two or three of the lambs, for the Lost Lambs activity. (Be sure these name tags are used.) Attach with straight pins or double-sided tape.

## Activity 1: What You've Always Wanted to Know About Being a Little Lamb's Mother and Were Afraid to Ask.

Give each guest a pen and a sheet of paper. Ask everyone to write her very best hint about enjoying a baby's first months. These can be funny or serious. Allow all who want to share their expertise on lamb raising to read their ideas aloud. Give answers to the mother-to-be for her baby's book.

## Activity 2: Bo Peep Has Lost Her Sheep

Dress a good-natured assistant as Bo Peep. (This can be a man if a willing volunteer is available and if you can stand the added hilarity.) A long skirt, sunbonnet, and a shepherd's crook from the church Christmas pageant makes a perfect costume.

As **Activity 1** is completed, Bo Peep will *burst* into the room. Wailing and with eyes shaded, she will look *everywhere* for her lost sheep. After a trip or two around the circle of guests, crying and inquiring about her little lost babies, ask guests to pardon the interruption, but will they please remove their name tags to see if their lamb is one of Bo Peep's missing ones? Give small gifts to those who are wearing the lambs with "Where am I?" on the back.

**Preparation for the Devotional Message:** Cut a 2 inch heart, a 2 inch smiling face, and a 3 inch church from white paper, as shown. Glue a loop of paper 1 inch x $1/4$ inch on the back of each one. Cut two yards of narrow apple green ribbon into three equal pieces. Slip a ribbon through the loops on the heart, face, and church, so they can be tied around the lamb's neck. Place each in a small gift box and tie with peach ribbon. Number boxes so mother will open gifts in correct sequence.

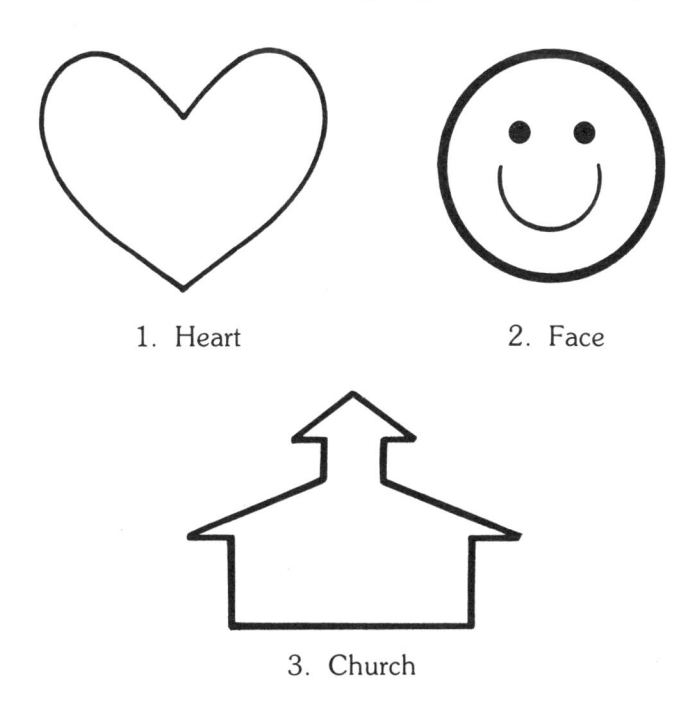

1. Heart

2. Face

3. Church

**Devotional Message: Mary Had a Little Lamb.**

(Mother-to-be's Name), I'm sure you've heard the nursery rhyme, "Mary had a little lamb. Its fleece was white as snow. And everywhere that Mary went, the lamb was sure to go." It won't be long until we can put *your* name in place of Mary's! Welcome to the occupation of Little Lamb Keepers. It's a fascinating field of endeavor.

As you know, little lambs are cute, cuddly, and lovable. They also are wobbly, helpless, and innocent. Your baby, in many ways, will remind you of a little lamb. I'm glad Psalm 23 contains a guide for the Little Lambs' mother.

You may be surprised to hear this Psalm used for baby care information. Remember, (Mother-to-be's Name), Scriptures which contain life principles are like your favorite maternity top. *You* wear it, then your *friend* wears it, and then *her* friend wears it. You *all* feel as if that top was made just for *you!* (Emphasize italicized words.) Great Scriptures *fit* everyone!.

Psalm 23 contains three wonderful principles which you can borrow for your little lamb, your baby. Taking the form of gifts, they include: Love, Laughter, and Life Ever-after! (Present the lamb from the serving table to the mother-to-be as a reminder, in days to come, of these gifts from Psalm 23.)

## Gift 1: Love

(Mother-to-be's Name), let's open the first gift. (Ask her to tie the heart around the lamb's neck.)

This little heart stands for *love*. Psalm 23:1 (NIV) tells us, "The Lord is my shepherd, I shall lack nothing."

Love is demonstrated by *good* shepherds and *good* mothers through meeting the needs of those dependent on them. One of the best ways you can fill your little lamb's needs is with your voice.

The shepherd's voice is known and loved by his sheep. They will follow no other voice because their shepherd lovingly meets their needs.

(Mother-to-be's Name), your little lamb will know your voice too. You'll be thrilled to see how quickly your baby recognizes your voice. You will speak, and he will know, *That's my mom!* Studies show that babies respond to and benefit from their parents' voices, even before birth.

After your child is born, experts recommend that you continue a running conversation with him, including him in whatever you are doing. For instance, when you're shopping in the supermarket, ask him, "What sounds good for lunch today, bananas and pineapple?" Other shoppers may look embarrassed and make a wide swing around your cart, but ignore them. You'll probably never see them again, but your baby will be your conversation buddy for years to come.

While your voice demonstrates love to your baby, listening to his voice shows you care for him, as well. Now, let's face it, a baby's first words are quite uniform: *"Waaagh!"* But, (Mother-to-be's Name), *"Waaagh"* means many things in baby language. Besides "I'm hungry, wet, or sleepy," it may also convey "I'm bored, lonely, or need a better location to watch you, Mother." Listen carefully, and your baby lamb will amaze you with the variety of messages he sends your way.

The exchange and blending of your voice with your child's can surpass any other communication system in the world. The reason behind this is clear: the transmission will be powered by love.

### Gift 2: Laughter

(Ask the mother-to-be to open the second gift and tie the smiling face around the lamb's neck.)

This second gift, a smiling face, represents *laughter*. Psalm 23:5 says, "You anoint my head with oil, my cup overflows." (Mother-to-be's Name), oil in Scripture is associated with the Holy Spirit and joy. People who are filled with God's Presence in the form of the Holy Spirit, can experience a tremendous amount of joy and love for life.

Joy, for many of us, bubbles out of our hearts as laughter. (Mother-to-be's Name), I hope you already like to laugh. *Laughter* makes being a baby lamb's mother much easier. When your baby wears more food on the outside of his face than you've spooned successfully inside, *laugh!* When you arrive at the pediatrician's office, and in your rush have put on two different shoes, *laugh!* When you discover your baby curled up in a position an adult could never negotiate, *laugh!* Find delight and humor in even the smallest, and most unplanned details of your little lamb's babyhood.

Babies respond to a happy, laughing mother like a duck takes to water. Remember you are on an adventure together. He'll be busy learning to be a little person. And you'll be attempting, if not your first mothering, at least one of your few tries at raising a baby from lambhood. If you can laugh instead of being afraid that you'll make a mistake and ruin him, you can form a bond of friendship for life.

### Gift 3: Life Ever-after

(Ask mother-to-be to open the third gift and tie the church around the lamb's neck. Add this to the heart and smiling face.)

This third gift, a church, represents *life ever-after*. Psalm 23:6 (NIV) says, "Surely goodness and love will follow me all the days of my life, and I will dwell in the house of the Lord forever".

(Mother-to-be's Name), the gift of life ever-after comes only from God, himself, as we accept Jesus Christ as our Savior. A child's picture of Heaven, however, often is drawn by his mother's attitude toward God's House on earth, the Church.

You can lead your child to love God's House in several ways. First of all, *live* Psalm 122:1 before him, "I rejoiced with those who said to me, '"Let us go to the house of the Lord'." You can do this in these ways.

1. Act happy to go to church each Sunday. You'll find that transporting a baby requires great organizational skills. Try putting everything you'll need to take to church by the front door on Saturday night, except the baby, of course.

2. Make friends with God's people. You'll gain wisdom and support from godly people to help you become a better parent. You'll also love God's house more because you are known, loved, and accepted there.

3. Show appreciation to the nursery attendants who care for your baby. Express frequent praise, and volunteer your help occasionally. The nursery workers will thank God *and* you for your thoughtfulness.

If you follow these guidelines, your little lamb will probably choose God's house as one of his favorite places to go. And best of all, (Mother-to-be's Name), you'll discover that a child who visits God's house regularly, often accepts God's gift of *life ever-after* at an early age.

**Conclusion:** (Hold the lamb, with the three gifts tied around its neck for everyone to see).

"Mary had a little lamb" and before long, (Mother-to-be's Name), you'll have a little lamb too. Communicate with your baby in *love*. Make your hearts sing together with *laughter*. And by modeling the joy you feel in God's house, encourage him to seek and find *life ever-after*.

**Prayer:** Dear Father, we thank You that the Shepherd's Psalm provides a path for (Mother-to-be's Name) to follow. We thank You for Jesus, the Good Shepherd, who walked before us as a perfect example. Help (Mother-to-be's Name) as she shares the gifts of love, laughter, and life ever-after with her little lamb, her new baby. In Jesus' name, amen."

Present the mother-to-be with a typed or handwritten copy of the devotional for the baby book.

**Open Gifts:** See Gift Opening Ideas on page 53.

**Refreshments:** Serve the main course when guests arrive. Serve dessert after the devotional message.
>    Breakfast Souffle (page 57)
>    Ambrosia
>    Spinach Salad
>    Carrot and Bran Muffins
>    Cherry Meringue Dessert (page 59)
>    Coffee and Tea (decaffeinated and regular)

# 7
# A Star Is Born

Theme verse: "You saw me before I was born and scheduled each day of my life before I began to breathe. Every day was recorded in your Book!" – Psalm 139:16 (The Living Bible)

**Decorations:** Choose a yellow and white color scheme to set the stage for the *star* who will soon be born. Use white table linens and yellow napkins. Place a large bouquet of daisies and greenery in the center of the table. Borrow a canvas Director's chair and decorate it with yellow and white balloons and streamers. Place matching balloon bouquets around the room.

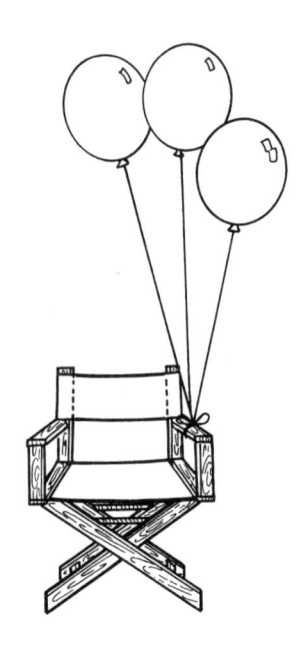

**Name Tags:** Cut tickets from heavy yellow paper 2" x 4½". Write *A Star Is Born* across top and *Admit One* across lower section with a black felt pen as shown. Add names with a green or a black pen. Attach with double-sided tape or straight pins.

> **A Star Is Born**
> **Nancy**
> **ADMIT ONE**

## Activity 1: Name Dropping

Name dropping is fun. Everyone enjoys letting others know that he knows celebrities! Since all the guests know this celebrity, the Mother-to-be, give them six minutes to pair off and name drop with the person seated next to them. Ask them to learn their partner's name, relationship to the mother-to-be, and any other interesting information. When time is completed, ask each guest to introduce her fellow name dropper and tell what she's learned about her. Keep the sharing relaxed and brief.

## Activity 2: Star Dusters

Cut out 5" yellow stars. Punch a small hole at the same point in each one. Give each guest a star and pen. Remind them that all mothers encounter days when stardust (or just plain dust) begins to collect on their stars. Ask them to write a favorite Scripture verse or prayer which (Mother-to-be's Name) can use as a star duster! Gather and read them aloud. String stars together with white yarn and present to the mother-to-be.

**Preparation for the Devotional Message:** Prepare three $5^1/_2$ inches x $8^1/_2$ inches Theater Flyers. Center and type the information found on page 44 on them.

## Devotional Message: A Star Is Born!

Press releases during the past few months have heralded the opening of a new play – your baby's life! We are balanced on

**Flyer #1:** Casting Call

**A STAR IS BORN**

Child needed for title role

A Great Theater of Life Production

---

**FLYER #2:** Script for

**A STAR IS BORN**

A New Play by: (Mother-to-be's Name)

---

**FLYER #3:** Performances Begin soon for

**A STAR IS BORN**

Starring: (Baby's Name)

Director: (Mother-to-be's Name)

---

**Flyers:**

44

the edges of our seats, anticipating that first performance – your baby's birth!

(Mother-to-be's Name), please take your place in this special chair because you will not only be the producer, you will be the director of your star's life as well.

(Bring in decorated, director's chair. Wait until mother-to-be is comfortably seated in it before you continue.)

Directors carry a far greater responsibility than most people realize. While the star performs in the limelight, the director works quietly in the wings.

As your child's mother, you will assume many of the same tasks as a director. You will help him find the right role. You will provide his script. You will influence his lifelong performance.

A mother in Scripture lived her directorship so supremely that she became a member of God's Hall of Fame. This exciting woman was Jochebed, the mother of Moses. We will look at her example and skill as a director.

**Jochebed's Daring Role Casting:** (Read Flyer #1 aloud and give to Mother-to-be.)

Psalm 139:16, (The Living Bible), tells us, "You saw me before I was born and scheduled each day of my life before I began to breathe. Every day was recorded in your Book!"

Moses' mother believed the message in this verse. In spite of her circumstances, she confidently claimed the role God had planned for her son.

Moses' birth, as you may remember, was not published in the Egyptian daily newspaper. Moses' arrival was kept a secret because Pharaoh thought he could keep the Hebrews in bondage if he killed all their baby boys.

Moses' mother acted on faith, not on Pharaoh's orders. She devised a plan and carried it through to help her son act out his starring role for God.

Hiding Moses in a waterproof basket, Jochebed set him afloat among the reeds in the Nile river. Moses' role of adventurous deliverer was defined at the tender age of three months! We'll leave Moses floating in the bulrushes while we talk about your turn at role casting.

**Your Turn at Role Casting:** (Mother-to-be's Name), you will soon help your star find his role in God's plan. Like Jochebed, your personality, interests, and life-style will reflect in your child's talents and motivation. You can introduce him to the wonders of God's world through music, art, and books. You can help him explore pebbles, raindrops, puppies, and leaves. God will use you, as his director, to help your star walk center stage for him.

**Jochebed Tries Her Hand at Scriptwriting:** (Read Flyer #2 aloud and give to Mother-to-be.)

(Mother-to-be's Name), a director not only matches a star with a role, she also provides him with a script. Sometimes the director even writes the script herself!

Today, many psychologists believe that from birth to five years, a child continually hears and records messages from his parents. These signals appear to be internalized and followed throughout the rest of his life, producing a life script.

Jochebed displayed great skill at this type of director-scriptwriting. Although she faced a difficult assignment in writing a script for Moses, Jochebed cleverly rose to the challenge. Let's hurry back to see if Moses is doing OK in the water.

Baby Moses, floating in his basket, was discovered one day by Pharaoh's daughter. Recognizing him as one of the condemned Hebrew children, she wanted to adopt him.

Fortunately, Cairo supermarkets did not stock formula and baby bottles. Pharaoh's daughter needed a *real* mother to nurse him!

Jochebed was ready for action. Moses' big sister, Miriam, jumped out of the bulrushes and offered her mother's help. During the next three years, or perhaps longer in that culture, Moses' mother cared lovingly for her own little son.

Can you imagine the script that Jochebed wrote on Moses' heart? A mother who was creative enough to camouflage and sail a bassinette must hve been a great *scriptwriter!* Courage, adventure, and resourcefulness flowed into Moses along with his mother's milk. Jochebed captured each moment and transcribed it on the heart of her son.

**How's Your Writing Hand?:** (Mother-to-be's Name), you will soon turn on the sights and sounds which will write the script for your little star's life. A few simple guidelines will ensure your success.

From his earliest days, tell him how very much you love him. Keep your messages of affirmation and acceptance soft, sweet, and strong. By words and actions, show him every day that he occupies a special place in your heart, and in God's, which nobody else can fill. Share your dreams for his life which fit his interests and abilities. Maintain a steady, consistent script which he can clearly read and follow.

**Jochebed's Star Performs:** A director's genius is only proven when the star, the role, and the script produce a grand performance! Moses made his mother's reputation as a director soar quickly.

Moses' drama-filled infancy had lapsed into an intermission as he left his mother's home to grow up in Pharaoh's palace. Treated to the finest food, clothing, and education, Moses could have forgotten his Jewish heritage, but his director's influence remained strong! His mother's example and teachings helped him remember his roots.

When his performance for God was scheduled, Moses defied the greatest power on earth, the Egyptians who had adopted him. He faced a burning bush, plagues, the Red Sea's parting, and God himself on Mt. Sinai. Moses performed as a star because his mother's directing had instilled her God in his heart!

**Your Star Will Perform Soon!:** (Read Flyer #3 aloud and give to mother-to-be.)

As opening night draws near, we look forward to this exciting event with you. We know that your directing, like Jochebed's, will receive rave reviews.

Those of us in the audience will applaud your star's flawless performances and pray when he misses a line here or there. With God's help and your directing, we're sure your star will become an all-time great!

**Prayer:** Dear Father, thank You for the privilege <u>(Mother-to-be's Name)</u> will have to direct her child's life in the years ahead. May Your Word and prayer give her guidance and strength. In Jesus' name, amen.

Present a typed or handwritten copy of the Devotional Message to the Mother-to-be for her baby's book.

**Open Gifts:** (See Gift Opening Ideas on page 53.)

**Refreshments:** Fresh Vegetable Tray (page 58)
                     Cheesecakes with Assorted Fruit Toppings
                     Sparkling White Grape Punch (page 56)
                     Coffee and Tea (decaffeinated and regular)

# Baby Shower Interview Questions

1. Where will your baby be born?
2. When is your baby's anticipated arrival date?
3. Have you chosen names?
   a) If so, can you share them?
   b) Do these names have special meaning?
   c) Will your child be named for someone?
4. Will your baby have a nickname?
5. Will someone help you at home after the baby arrives?
6. Describe the colors and/or theme of your baby's nursery.
7. How many grandparents and great-grandparents will your baby have?
8. How many aunts, uncles, and cousins are in your baby's awaiting fan club?
9. Have you eaten any strange combinations of food the past months?
10. Upon hearing the words, "It's time to go to the hospital," will your husband be calm and controlled or frantic and frazzled?
11. What word best describes your feelings about the past nine months?
12. What word best describes your feelings about the next nine months?
13. Name your husband's best qualities for being a great father.
14. What past experience do you expect to find most helpful for you as a mother?

15. Do you have a lullabye prepared to sing to your baby?
16. Which relative will show her friends the most baby pictures?
17. Which relative will spoil your baby most?
18. Which hobby do you expect your baby to pursue at an early age?
19. Is there a Scripture verse which is meaningful as you anticipate your child's birth?
20. Have you chosen a Scripture verse as a theme for your new life which you, your husband, and your baby will share?

# Bridal Shower Interview Questions

1. Who is most responsible for your meeting (Groom)?
2. What was (Groom) doing when you first saw him?
3. How long was it from your first meeting to your first date?
4. Where did you go on your first date?
5. Describe your most humorous date.
6. Describe your most unusual date.
7. Describe your most romantic date.
8. When did you first realize this was true love?
9. Where were you when (Groom) proposed?
10. Give the names of your wedding attendants.
11. Where are you going on your honeymoon?
12. Where will you and (Groom) work?
13. Where will you live?
14. Where will you attend church?
15. What personality trait do you most admire in (Groom)?
16. What personality trait do you tease him about most?
17. What personality trait do you have most in common?
18. Choose one word to describe your courtship.
19. Describe your favorite kind of day to spend together.
20. Which level of cooking does (Groom) practice?
    a. Gourmet   b. Meat and potatoes   c. Survival
21. Which level of cooking do you practice?
    a. Gourmet   b. Meat and potatoes   c. Survival

22. If you are participating in sports with (Groom), such as tennis or golf, do you:
    a. try to win?   b. let him win?   c. just have fun?
23. Are you both morning people, both night people, or one of each?
24. What song, sacred or secular, do you want to represent the theme of your marriage?
25. Which Scripture do you want to follow in your marriage?
26. What schedule do you follow for cleaning your house or apartment?
    a. Once a week   b. Once a month   c. When you move
27. What schedule does (Groom) follow for cleaning his house or apartment?
    a. Once a week   b. Once a month   c. When he moves

# Gift Opening Ideas

1. Have the guest of honor sit in a special chair, trimmed with flowers, balloons, or streamers. This will create a center of interest for other guests to watch.
2. Seat family members near the bride or mother-to-be so they can see and hear her as she opens gifts.
3. Select someone to hand gifts to the honoree.
4. Choose a person to list each gift, its giver, and a brief description of the gift on a separate record.
5. Provide scissors, a knife, and other sharp tools to help the bride or mother-to-be open gifts more easily.
6. Ask someone to arrange bows from gifts in a bouquet by pulling ribbons through a paper plate, prepared with a three-inch slit in the center.
7. Pass gifts to guests or place on a table for later viewing.
8. Show interest, as the hostess, in each gift as it is opened.
9. If there is a large number of gifts, pause after a while to serve punch or refreshments.
10. Allow time for the bride or mother-to-be to express thanks to guests for coming, as well as for their gifts.

# Recipes

# Punch Recipes

### Sparkling White Grape Punch

   32 ounces white grape juice
   Two 2-liter bottles of 7up

Mix chilled grape juice and 7up in punch bowl.
Add crushed ice and lemon slices.
Makes about 30  5-ounce servings.

### Sunshine Punch

   12 ounces frozen orange juice
   12 ounces frozen lemonade (optional)
   One 2-liter bottle of 7up.

Prepare juice according to instructions.
Add 1/2 cup sugar, if desired. Add 7up, crushed ice, and orange or lemon slices.
Makes about 35  5-ounce servings.

# Casserole Recipe

### Breakfast Souffle

8 slices white bread (remove crusts and cube)
1 pound grated sharp cheese
1 1/2 pounds sausage (cooked and crumbled)

Place bread in a buttered 9" x 13" casserole. Top with sausage and cheese.
Mix the following ingredients:
    4 eggs, beaten      3/4 teaspoon mustard
    2 1/2 cups milk      1/2 teaspoon salt
Pour mixture over casserole. Refrigerate overnight.
Before baking, mix and pour over casserole:
    1 can cream of mushroom soup      1/2 cup milk
    2 cups fresh mushrooms, sliced
Bake at 300 degrees for 1 1/2 hours. Cut in squares. Serves 10.


# Dip Recipes

### Spinach Dip

1 package frozen chopped spinach (thaw and squeeze dry)
8 ounces cream cheese
8 ounces sour cream
1 can water chestnuts, finely chopped, drained
1 package dry vegetable soup mix
2 tablespoons mayonnaise

Soften cream cheese. Mix remaining ingredients.
Serve with raw vegetables.

### Trip Through the Garden Dip

2 tablespoons chopped green onion      1 cup sour cream
2 tablespoons minced watercress      1 garlic clove, crushed
2 tablespoon minced tarragon      1/4 teaspoon salt
1 cup plain yogurt      1/8 teaspoon pepper

Combine herbs and seasonings. Add 1 cup plain yogurt and sour cream. Mix well. Serve with raw vegetables.

## Crab Dip

8 ounces sour cream
3 ounces softened cream cheese
1 cup crab meat
1 tablespoon worcestershire sauce
1 teaspoon minced onion
1 teaspoon lemon juice

Mix ingredients and chill.

*Vegetable Tray Suggestions:* Prepare crisp carrot and celery strips, cauliflower and broccoli flowerets, cucumber, zucchini and jicama slices, cherry tomatoes, radishes, and mushrooms. Arrange on ruffled lettuce. Garnish with parsley.

## Rosy Posy Dip

8 ounces vanilla yogurt
1/2 cup cranberry-orange relish
1/4 teaspoon ground nutmeg
1/4 teaspoon ground ginger

Combine yogurt and relish. Add spices. Chill well.

## Hawaiian Adventure Dip

1 large jar marshmallow cream
2 teaspoon grated orange peel
8 ounces cream cheese
dash ginger

Soften cream cheese. Blend in remaining ingredients. Serve with fruit.

## Easy Way Out Dip

2 cups brown sugar
2 cups sour cream

Place brown sugar and sour cream in individual bowls. Guests can dip fruit in sour cream, then in brown sugar.

*Fruit Tray Suggestions:* Prepare strawberries, kiwi fruit, pineapple, melons, and blueberries. Arrange on a crystal platter. Garnish with parsley, mint leaves, or flowers.

## Desserts

### Cherry Meringue Dessert

Meringue:
- 6 egg whites
- 3/4 teaspoon cream of tartar
- 2 cups sugar
- 1 cup walnuts
- 2 cups *soda* crackers
- 2 teaspoons vanilla

Beat egg whites until they peak but not until dry. Gradually add cream of tartar and sugar. Beat until glossy. Add walnuts (broken in large pieces), soda crackers (broken in chunks), and vanilla. Pour into 9" x 13" buttered glass baking dish. Bake at 350 degrees for 25 minutes (no longer). Cool. Refrigerate.

Topping:
Before serving, swirl a large carton of whipped topping or 1 pint of whipping cream, whipped and sweetened, over top of meringue. Leave 1 1/2" around the edge of meringue without topping. Drizzle a can of cherry pie filling over the top. (Blueberry pie filling or fresh strawberries may be substituted.) Cut in squares to serve. (This dessert looks especially impressive in a silver serving dish.)

## Chocolate Dream Dessert

Crust:
    1/2 cup margarine
    3/4 cup chopped walnuts or pecans
    1 cup flour
    1/4 cup brown sugar

Mix and pat in 9" by 13" pan. Bake 15 minutes at 350 degrees. Cool.

Layer 1:
    8 ounces cream cheese
    1 cup powdered sugar
    1/2 of 12 ounce carton of whipped topping.

Soften cream cheese. Mix with sugar and whipped topping. Spread over cooled crust.

Layer 2:
    3 packages chocolate instant pudding mix
    4 cups milk
    1 teaspoon vanilla

Beat with rotary mixer. Spoon on top of first layer.

Layer 3:
    Add remainder of whipped topping. Sprinkle 1/3 cup of chopped nuts. Refrigerate. Serves 15.
*Any flavor of pudding may be used.

## Lemon Angel Food Dessert

    1 angel food cake mix
    2 cups pineapple juice
    6-ounce package lemon gelatin
    2 cups orange juice
    1 cup sugar
    1 12-ounces whipped topping

Bake angel food cake. Freeze slightly. Cut cake in 1" cubes. Place cake pieces in buttered 9" x 13" glass baking dish. Heat pineapple juice. Add sugar and blend well. Add gelatin stirring until dissolved. Add orange juice. Chill until mixture begins to thicken. Beat whipping cream, sweeten if you like, and fold into gelatin mixture. Pour over cake pieces. Stir gently to cover cake pieces. Refrigerate overnight.

    Garnish with whipped cream and mandarin orange slices. Serves 12-15.

## Fudge Lover's Cake

1 fudge cake mix
1 cup chocolate chips
1/2 cup chopped walnuts

Prepare cake according to package instructions. Add 1/2 cup chocolate chips to batter. Spread in waxed-paper-lined 9" x 13" pan. Sprinkle remainder of chocolate chips and the nuts over batter. Bake at 350 degrees for 30-35 minutes. Cool 10 minutes. Loosen sides of cake. Cover with waxed paper. Turn on to paper-lined cookie sheet and then on to doily-covered tray.

*Icing:* Melt 1/4 cup butter or margarine. Add 2 to 3 tablespoons hot coffee, 2 tablespoons cocoa, 1 teaspoon vanilla, and 1/8 teaspoon salt. Beat in 1/2 pound powdered sugar. Add more coffee if needed. Icing can also be thinned by heating a few seconds. Drizzle icing over cake.

## Chocoholic Layer Cake

2 fudge cake mixes            2 cups chocolate chips

Prepare cake mixes according to package instructions. Add chocolate chips (optional). Divide batter in four 9" layer pans, lined with waxed paper. Bake at 350 degrees 30-35 minutes. Cool 10 minutes. Turn out on waxed-paper-lined plates, top up, to cool.

*Icing:*
  1 cup butter or margarine, softened      6 tablespoons hot coffee
  2 pounds powdered sugar                  2 tablespoon cream
  6 tablespoon Cocoa                       1 chopped walnuts
  1/4 teaspoons salt

Beat softened butter, cocoa, salt, and coffee together. Beat in powdered sugar. Add cream until icing reaches easy spreading consistency. Beat well.
To assemble:
Place first layer on round paper doily, topside *down,* on cake plate. Add icing to cover layer and 1/4 cup of walnuts. Add 2 additional

layers, topside *up,* icing, and walnuts. Ice sides of cake. Refrigerate. Cut cake in thin slices to serve.

Place remaining layer on a plate. Ice and sprinkle with nuts. Leave at home for your family, share with a friend, or wrap in foil and freeze for later use.

### Pineapple-Carrot Cake

| | |
|---|---|
| 2 cups sugar | 2 teaspoons Cinnamon |
| 1 1/2 cups vegetable oil | 4 eggs |
| 8 1/2 ounces crushed pineapple (undrained) | |
| 2 cups flour | 1 1/2 cups flaked coconut |
| 2 teaspoons baking powder | 1 cup chopped walnuts |
| 1 1/2 teaspoons baking soda | 2 cups grated carrots |
| 1 teaspoon salt | |

In mixer bowl, beat sugar and oil. Beat eggs and add to mixture, beating well. Add flour, baking powder, baking soda, salt, and cinnamon. Stir in carrots, pineapple, nuts, and coconut. Divide batter into three 9" layer pans, lined with waxed paper. Bake at 350 degrees for 30-35 minutes. Cool 10 minutes Turn out of pans on waxed paper to cool, topside up.

*Icing:*

| | |
|---|---|
| 1/2 cup butter or margarine | dash salt |
| 8 ounces cream cheese, softened | 1 teaspoon vanilla |
| 1 pound powdered sugar | |

Cream butter or margarine, softened cream cheese, and vanilla. Beat in powdered sugar. Beat well. Place first layer on doily-covered cake plate. Spread 1/3 icing on *top* of layer. Add, and ice, second and third layers in the same way. Leave sides of cake plain. You may sprinkle 1/4 cup chopped nuts on top of each layer, if desired. Refrigerate until serving time. Serve in small slices.

### Cake Making Hints:
*Cool cakes topside up. Use the double flip method to remove cakes from pans. Loosen sides of cake with a knife. Place a piece of waxed paper over the top of cake and also on top of a cookie sheet. Place the cookie sheet over the cake, and, holding both firmly, turn over

quickly. Then place another paper-covered cookie sheet on the overturned cake and flip back so the cake is topside up again.
*Assemble layer cakes by placing the first layer topside down and the second layer topside up.
*Paper doilies add a professional touch.
*Use pedestal-type cake plates for added dramatic effect.
*Paper doilies, mentioned above, simplify sliding cakes to pedestal plates just before serving.

## Sherbet or Ice Cream Bouquet:

Choose colorful flavors, such as lemon, raspberry, and lime sherbet, or pistachio and peppermint ice cream. Using an ice cream dipper, scoop large, single scoops and place on waxed-paper-covered cookie sheets. Cover well with plastic wrap and freeze until firm. When firm, place an additional cover of aluminum foil.

*Serving:* At serving time, arrange the various flavors in a chilled glass or silver bowl to resemble a bouquet. Encircle the bowl with greenery. Add sprigs of mint throughout the bouquet. Let guests serve themselves.